STOP My Childhood From Drowning!
39 Lessons From A Child Experiencing Divorce

By E. R. Reid

STOP My Childhood From Drowning!

STOP My Childhood From Drowning!
39 Lessons From A Child Experiencing Divorce

By E. R. Reid

FRUITION
WWW.FRUITIONONLINE.COM

"Preparing Minds For Action"

**Fruition Online Publishing
Raleigh, NC**

Copyright © 2003, Eleanor R. White

Cover Design By Keith Scott,
Keith Scott Designs
Edited By Patrick Taggart

All Rights Reserved. This Book, Or Parts Thereof, May Not Be Reproduced In Any Form Without Permission.

Published By Fruition Online Publishing
702 Oberlin Road, Suite 150
Raleigh, NC 27605
www.fruitiononline.com

Library of Congress Cataloging-In-Publication Data

ISBN 0-9712079-3-3

Printed In The United States Of America

Contents

Acknowledgements   xiii
Foreword   xv
Introduction   xvii

Lessons And Perspectives   21

1. I Don't Understand What Just Happened
2. I Feel Afraid And Alone
3. I Feel Angry
4. I Don't Have The Same Problems With Mom/Dad That You Have. So Don't Bust My Bubble!
5. I Feel Safest When We're All Together
6. Smile, So I Know You're Not Disappointed With Me
7. Listen When I Speak, Don't Ignore Me
8. Remember, I'm Still Just A Kid
9. Don't Stop Playing With Me
10. Please Don't Treat Me Like I'm Not Here
11. Stop Spending So Much Time Away From Me
12. I Need Friends And I Want Them To Like You

Contents

13. My Disobedience Is Sometimes Just My Frustration

14. I Depend On You To Help Me Grow

15. I Love To Help Out, But ...

16. I Depend On You To Be There For Me

17. Please Do Something Other Than Work

18. Please Sit Down And Eat Dinner With Me

19. I Want To Spend Less Time With Babysitters

20. Please Don't Yell At Me When I Make Mistakes

21. I'm Loud When I Play Because That's What Kids Do

22. Please Say Yes, Sometimes

23. Let Me Know When I Do A Good Job

24. Remember That I Have Needs, Too

25. I Want You To Try To Work It Out

26. Work It Out Or Work Together

Contents

27. Too Much Change Really Scares Me

28. Sometimes I Feel It Is My Fault

29. Please Let Me Know That You Still Love Me

30. I Want To Know That You're All Right

31. I Need To Be Reassured, Constantly

32. We Don't Need To Spend Money To Have A Lot Of Fun

33. More Family Can Be A Good Thing If...

34. We Are All Still Family

35. I Want To Stay With You Forever

36. I Love To See You Smile

37. Be Patient With Me. There's A Lot I Have To Figure Out

38. I May Feel Sad From Time To Time

39. Always Remember That I Love You More Than Anything Else

Conclusion   **101**

Acknowledgements

To Eric and Kennedy,

Thank you for your patience and love.

Foreword

E. R. Reid has gained great insight into the world of children as a committed mother, community leader, business executive, and volunteer. She has established a reputation as one who understands issues affecting people and potential ways to improve the quality of their lives. I have come to respect her as a dedicated board member for Communities In Schools of Wake County, and have seen her apply this insight when working with the children who benefit from our program. She makes sacrifices daily on behalf of these under-served or at-risk children who are sometimes victims of divorce.

Those in the many stages of divorce can benefit from this guide presented from the child's perspective. Those of us who are unfamiliar with the struggles of divorce and the impact it has on children will learn through the creative presentation of the issues. E.R. Reid presents "real life" situations children endure, and the book puts the reader in a face-to-face conversation with the child; revealing not only their point of view but the emotions that go hand in hand with their struggles.

She presents lessons and perspectives that can be used by parents, guardians, teachers, and all caring adults. She guides us through a meaningful process that empowers the child with a voice and their family with a guide for reinstating the family unit.

Children who are victims of divorce struggle for balance, stability, and understanding in their lives.

They are challenged with the realities of loneliness, confusion, and disillusionment through no fault of their own. For all who are serious about making a difference for a child, this book is a must read. It is engaging, informative, and instructional.

Dr. Classy Preston
Author, <u>Shaping Character in At-Risk Children</u>

Introduction

No one wants to be a statistic, at least not one that society equates with failure. Unfortunately, far too many of us end up as part of the divorce statistic, and it has become so commonplace that it has almost lost its stigma. Most discussion about it today is centered on its causes, attempts to repair the breach and the after-effects to the adults involved. Even though the traumatic effects on children are recognized, the impact of divorce on them is primarily discussed as an aside.

I was inspired to write this book because I realized that the needs of our children in this situation should be deliberately attended to. Children are often overwhelmed with information. Because of this, we as parents must provide guidance and examples to teach a child how to manage and use information as they grow.

Anyone that has gone through divorce knows how painful and disorienting it can be. It is a major life change to break a bond, divide a home and step out to rebuild another, often on your own. Emotional pain requires time for healing and for gathering physical and psychological strength. This must be done while one continues to do what was necessary to sustain life even before the divorce.

When children are added to this equation, the transition becomes significantly more complex. Because now you are not only responsible for standing on your own two feet; you must also help at least one other human being adjust who may not have the maturity to make even the simplest transitions for themselves. You, as the parent, are caring for someone who is now even more dependent on you than before. Our children may become more dependent, in part, because they are experiencing something that refutes something else they had already learned and come to rely upon. However, you as the human being are finding that it takes enough effort just to keep yourself moving forward.

At some point in the divorce process, I had to stop and take a hard look at my children, my interactions with them, and myself. What made me stop was lifting my head out of the sand long enough to notice my children looking strangely at me. I have spent years empathizing with business clients and helping them to improve their companies. With my clients, I am able to adeptly analyze their complexity and chaos, pinpoint the driving factors of their issues, and develop solutions that bring about success. My challenge was to apply that same understanding and attentiveness to my own young children to keep them from forfeiting the many treasures of childhood.

In the pages that follow, I share the results of taking an empathetic view to my own children and others that I observed going through divorce. I then offer my perspectives as a parent who knows what a challenge it is to find healing for oneself, help dependents heal, and still carry out with excellence the responsibilities of childrearing.

There are 39 lessons mentioned here. No doubt many of you can add your own. But I offer these as a starting point for understanding what may be going on in the hearts and minds of our children, and to help us find a way to balance their needs with ours. This way, the entire family comes through the divorce with as few losses as possible and perhaps even greater gain.

I recommend that you read the lessons before reading the corresponding perspective. The lessons are written in a child's voice, as they are articulations of what a child may feel but cannot fully express. The perspective is intended to provide additional insight into the lessons and discuss alternatives we may have as parents to assist our children with that particular issue.

Although this book was specifically written to address the needs of families that experience divorce, I believe it holds insights for single parents and those still making the effort to improve their marriages in order to avoid divorce. I believe you will find this book useful for opening discussions in your own homes – discussions that bring about healing and reconnection.

Sons are a heritage from the Lord, children a reward from Him.

Psalm 127:3[1]

---

[1]. Scripture taken from the Holy Bible, NEW INTERNATIONAL VERSION®. Copyright © 1973, 1978, 1984 International Bible Society. All rights reserved throughout the world. Used by permission of International Bible Society.

Lesson #1

"I Don't Understand What Just Happened"

All I know is that I was going along just fine. I was getting used to life as it was. I was learning new things, getting used to some things and feeling the need to continue to try new things just to see how far I could go before you pulled me back. I was comfortable with our family life. Good or bad, it's what I was used to and came to expect. Both of you were my security blanket. If all else failed, I knew I had the two of you.

Now, one of you is gone. Things are different around the house. Our routines are no longer routines. Instead of seeing both of you every day, I only see one of you, maybe. Why do I have to "visit" to see the other of you? I thought we were family, a unit that always sticks together. Why are you alone in your bed when I go to you in the morning? Why is only one of you here to tuck me in and say goodnight? Why is it such a big deal, now, to get both of you to support my activities? I feel different, home feels different and I don't know what it means.

Perspective #1

Divorce. I don't think any of us enter into marriage with the expectation that it will end in divorce. But for a variety of reasons, too many of our marriages do. For a childless couple, parting may be relatively uncomplicated. But for a couple with children the probability of significant emotional and physical heartache increases.

Children are often the last to know, and they usually don't find out until right before or shortly after one of the parents leaves the home. Rightfully, we go out of our way to protect our children from the discoveries, arguments, and resolution attempts that precede a divorce. But often we neglect to recognize the sudden shock and confusion that comes with experiencing a major change in the final hour.

Because children can't process information in the same manner as mature adults, they may be dazed and confused for an extended period of time without our even knowing it. One of the most valuable things I found that we can do is to stay tuned-in to their needs, asking them specific questions about their feelings regarding the divorce and speaking truthfully about the changes they have experienced and will experience in the future.

Lesson #2

"I Feel Afraid And Alone"

When I'm at home now I feel a little empty, like something's missing. Sometimes I walk around the house trying to find it. But I never do. I miss the feeling I had when you both were here filling the space. It's scary with just one of you because I feel like the other of you is lost. You both mean so much to me that losing either one of you makes me feel alone.

I don't know how to comfort myself. Sometimes, I try not thinking about it by playing or focusing real hard on a book, TV, or my music. But when I get tired of that, I look around and one of you is still gone. I'm not sure how to fill the space you left open. The only thing that can fill this space and make me feel better is something that I can rely on. I really hope it's you.

Perspective #2

Usually, one of the last things you want to do when you've separated from your partner is to see them frequently. Although part of you does want to see that person – after all, the bond is not completely broken yet – actually seeing them again may bring back all the hurt and/or anger associated with the reasons you divorced.

As adults, we need to heal and adjust to a new way of life. Unfortunately, I have found that when children are involved you don't have the luxury of taking your time to do it. Nor do you have the luxury of doing it exactly the way you would like to for yourself. There is a huge void left when one of you departs the home. It may be more peaceful, but there is still emptiness when one's presence is gone.

I found that allowing the child to interact with each parent as much as he or she desires helps to minimize their sense of loss and disconnection. As much as we may not want to, working together right after the divorce is essential to helping children adjust to their new environment. Working together early on and knowing how we're going to help our children gives us greater freedom in doing what we need to do in order to help ourselves.

Lesson #3

"I Feel Angry"

Okay. Things don't seem to be going back to normal. I was hoping that this was just temporary, like a dream, and you'd be back by now. Every time you come to "visit" me or pick me up I think this might be the time you decide to stay. I keep hoping there will be bags in your hands, which I would gladly help you carry.

But with each trip you make to see me, my mind gets more used to you just making a trip. I don't like that I'm getting used to this new routine. I want to fight to change it back. Isn't the big smile on my face when you're together a clue? When I cry for one of you when I'm with the other of you, isn't that a hint I'd rather be with both of you? What else can I possibly do!?

Nothing I do is working. I'm angry because I can't seem to win no matter how hard I try. I'm mad because I'm starting to accept that this is the way things are. I'm starting to accept defeat. What was real and good to me is now a dream that I can't make real again.

Perspective #3

As parents we can adjust relatively quickly to changes in our life, especially if we have the benefit of seeing them coming. We adjust but our children are often still processing the event.

As I began to adjust, I watched one of my otherwise sweet children begin to act out in anger as he began to accept that one of us was no longer calling our place home. He would get frustrated with the simplest of things. He became less interested in playing with other children and began to retreat to a place within himself where it appeared no one else was invited.

What helped him make a better adjustment was my persistence in engaging his attention through conversation and play. Although he was young, I had to ask him questions that would allow him to express his thoughts, as he was obviously drawing conclusions. My goal was to make sure he drew the right conclusions from the barrage of new information he was experiencing from the divorce. I couldn't erase all of his disappointment and quite honestly I couldn't erase all of my own. But together we found a way to make it better so we could get on with our lives.

Lesson #4

"I Don't Have The Same Problem With Mom/Dad That You Have. So Don't Bust My Bubble"

I don't understand why you don't like each other anymore. I look at each of you, and although you do it in different ways, you bring me happiness. Mom, I feel better when you cuddle me and tell me everything will be all right. Dad, you make me feel stronger. You both make sure I have what I need and sometimes, the things I want. You both make me feel like I have nothing to worry about when you're around. I admire both of you.

So, it's confusing to me when I hear you say bad things about each other or make bad faces when you talk about each other. I hear and see it all! Remember when you taught me everything about strangers and "bad" people? Well, now you're talking about each other as though you were one of them. How can this be when I love you so much? I need to trust you both. I don't want to lose *everything*! Don't try to change my mind with things I don't understand. Let me love each of you for who you are to *me* at this point in my life.

Perspective #4

Divorce is a humiliating experience for most of us. One of the hardest things is telling our family, friends, and co-workers. How can you tell everyone "you failed"? In an effort to overcome those feelings of failure, we may experience a persistent urge to blame the other partner. If they hadn't done this or that, or if they weren't like this or that, we could have worked it out. Vocalizing these feelings may, for a moment or two, feel therapeutic and liberating.

But often we forget that our children, though not oblivious to all of our marital interactions, don't fully understand what they observe nor do they always use that information to make judgments about us. Their judgments are based on their own experiences. For the most part, they love and think the world of both of us because they've found in us love, provision, and protection.

Exposing them to our adult disappointments, which they are not mature enough to fully understand, only heightens their confusion and erodes their trust in both parents. I found that you have to let them believe what they've come to believe about each of you until they are ready to make new judgments based on their own experience and maturity.

Lesson #5

"I Feel Safest When We're All Together"

I'm starting to get used to all of this. Being with at least one of you most of the time is better than being with neither of you at all. But I must say I really enjoy the times when we are all together in the same place, even if it's just for a few minutes. I don't feel as hopeful, but just for a moment that scary empty space starts to fill in again. Every time you sit together and talk to each other while I'm around that space fills in just a little bit more.

You see, I'm connected to you both. There's just something about us all being together in the same room. I know you're not staying, but these brief visits really help me to feel more secure with this new way of doing things, especially when you're being nice to each other.

Perspective #4

Divorce is a humiliating experience for most of us. One of the hardest things is telling our family, friends, and co-workers. How can you tell everyone "you failed"? In an effort to overcome those feelings of failure, we may experience a persistent urge to blame the other partner. If they hadn't done this or that, or if they weren't like this or that, we could have worked it out. Vocalizing these feelings may, for a moment or two, feel therapeutic and liberating.

But often we forget that our children, though not oblivious to all of our marital interactions, don't fully understand what they observe nor do they always use that information to make judgments about us. Their judgments are based on their own experiences. For the most part, they love and think the world of both of us because they've found in us love, provision, and protection.

Exposing them to our adult disappointments, which they are not mature enough to fully understand, only heightens their confusion and erodes their trust in both parents. I found that you have to let them believe what they've come to believe about each of you until they are ready to make new judgments based on their own experience and maturity.

Lesson #5

"I Feel Safest When We're All Together"

I'm starting to get used to all of this. Being with at least one of you most of the time is better than being with neither of you at all. But I must say I really enjoy the times when we are all together in the same place, even if it's just for a few minutes. I don't feel as hopeful, but just for a moment that scary empty space starts to fill in again. Every time you sit together and talk to each other while I'm around that space fills in just a little bit more.

You see, I'm connected to you both. There's just something about us all being together in the same room. I know you're not staying, but these brief visits really help me to feel more secure with this new way of doing things, especially when you're being nice to each other.

Perspective #5

Everyone's divorce circumstance is different. But for the most part you have two fairly decent adults who just couldn't find a way to walk together in love and commitment.

In divorce, I have found that it is the child who has the most to overcome and the hardest time healing. Most children don't yet understand how the world works or at least why the adults run things like they do. But what they do know and are able to take comfort in is their connection to their parents.

Though you may not be predisposed to long visits in your home with your former partner, it may be useful to the child to observe you having a brief and friendly conversation when one of you comes to pick the child up. It reassures them of their own conviction that you're both good people and that although the two of you are no longer connected, they are still connected to each of you.

Lesson #6

"Smile, So I Know You're Not Disappointed With Me"

I look to you all the time. But with this new change, I look at you a lot more than I used to. I especially look at the way you look at me. What does it mean when you give me that blank stare? What does it mean when I try to catch your eye with a smile and you look right past me? What does it mean when you stare at me with great sadness in your eyes?

Sometimes when I go to hug you I don't feel your warmth like I used to. I'm sorry that I hurt you, if I did. When I don't see your smile, I try to fix what I may be doing wrong. See? I'm picking up after myself, I finished my homework without you having to tell me, I turned the TV down, I'm sitting quietly reading a book. Can I get one smile? Just a smile once and a while will make me feel really good.

Perspective #6

Life post-divorce can be demanding and hectic. Not only are you trying to overcome its emotional impact, but physically your responsibilities have changed if you are the parent with whom the children live. Now instead of two of you working together, you have to do everything on your own. It is a challenge to get healing for yourself and still look out for someone else – someone who really needs you.

You do need to spend time thinking about all that you've experienced including your ultimate decision to make the break. Sometimes during this process we are completely oblivious to the expressions on our faces or our demeanor as we go about doing what has to be done. But our children see us even though we may forget to see them. Our challenge, then, is to hold onto that part of ourselves that makes us good parents while we work through this life change. We must manage our new circumstances to the benefit our children and ourselves without being overcome by the change.

Lesson #7

"Listen When I Speak, Don't Ignore Me!"

Excuse me! This is the third time I've tried to tell you this! Don't you see me standing right behind you? I keep talking to you but you keep going like you don't hear me. Your eyes look so intense as you focus on your work around the house. I keep trying to have a conversation with you, but you are too hard to reach. I tell you things and when you do respond it's with a, "yea, okay" then you tune me out again. Did you even hear what I said?

Maybe that's just the way we communicate now. I've since tried it a few times, myself. You know when you have called me over and over but I don't answer? I'm not trying to be rude, but that just seems to be the way I communicate now. Like you, you almost have to knock me over before I come out of myself enough to hear you talking to me.

Perspective #7

It is easy to become so engrossed in our thoughts that we block out noises of any kind. I've learned that we can train ourselves to hear nothing other than what we want to hear. After the trauma of a divorce it's natural to put on a protective "cloak" to keep anything you don't want from piercing the veil and getting in.

Unfortunately for our children, if we "cloak" ourselves they are left on the outside along with everyone and everything else. While we are undercover, who is on the outside protecting them? While we are inward-focused, who is taking the outward view to monitor what is going on in their lives? By the same token, how can you reach out and express your affection for them?

As a divorced parent, healing has to be a family process. Not ours first and then the children's. It should be a collaborative and inclusive effort led by us.

Lesson #8

"Remember, I'm Still Just A Kid"

It's obvious that there's a lot going on much of which I still don't understand. I notice but I don't always know what to do about it. So, I do what I know how to do, which is be a kid. I try to have fun, play with my friends, and get into all sorts of things around the house.

But with almost everything I do you tell me to stop, be quiet or go do something else. If I did everything the way you're telling me to, all I'd do is wake up, get dressed, eat breakfast, go to school, come home, do my homework, eat my dinner, get cleaned up, and go to bed until I wake up again the next morning. I know you're tired a lot more than you used to be and you don't like loud noises or a lot of movement. Yet there's something inside pushing me to try more, look at more, and feel more. I'm not trying to disobey you. I think I'm just being a kid.

Perspective #8

Most adults have learned how to focus and prepare their environment to accomplish a task. There are few tasks more complex than figuring out how to best bring healing to your family while continuing to fulfill your daily responsibilities. Ideally, we would use our time at home to do this. But our children are still true to who they are. Ideally, it would be peaceful and quiet while you were processing your thoughts. Ideally, you would set a plan for what actions you each should take during the evening in order to get closer to that place of resolve.

But children don't work that way. An ideal planning environment for us is often the exact opposite of the ideal living environment for our children. They need to release their energy and find even simple reasons to laugh because laughter makes them feel better. Again, we have to adjust our norms to fit what is best for the entire in-home family rather than battling over whose environment should win out. Each family has to find that place of compromise or balance so that no one gets short-changed in the healing process.

Lesson #9

"Don't Stop Playing With Me"

Remember when before all this happened you both liked to play games with me and try to make me smile? Remember when you went out of your way to take me to the park and maybe out for ice cream? Remember all the times you would come home with a surprise toy that I didn't even ask you for? I LOVED all of that! But I didn't love it because I got to play on the rides, or pick a new ice cream flavor, or even add a new toy to my collection.

I loved it because I got to spend special time with you. When I'm at the park playing with the other kids I feel special knowing my parent is sitting over there with all the other parents. I loved knowing you were watching me play and would be there in no time flat if I started to fall. I loved watching us all lick our ice cream cones together with you watching mine melt down the side of the cone and me watching yours do the same thing. I loved it when you took the time to teach me the rules of every new game and then played it with me at least three times before going to bed. You are the best playmate I've ever known. Please, don't stop playing with me.

Perspective #9

Things can get emotionally intense even after a divorce is final. It becomes hard to enjoy even a beautiful sunny day because many of us equate a happy life to having a partner. This is an issue many of us have to work through post-divorce: how to disconnect the association between enjoying life and having a partner.

Children don't necessarily need to make the disassociation, however. As long as at least one of us is in their lives, they should be able to look forward to having playful interactions with us. Quite honestly, this is not only satisfying for them but it's quite helpful for us as we find other ways to appreciate life without our former partners.

Lesson #10

"Please Don't Treat Me Like I'm Not Here"

Sometimes I just stop and watch you. You work around the house, cook, clean, and sit down to read a book or watch television. Many times you'll walk right by me without even looking me in the face. Sometimes I feel like I'm just another item on your "to do" list. You know, another object that you have to clean up and put in its proper place.

But guess what? I'm very much alive and I live right here with you. I would like a little conversation from time to time about things that have nothing to do with chores or my responsibilities. A smile or a "how's it going" when you pass me in the hallway would be nice, too. I know your mind is on a lot of different things and I think you're trying to find a way to be happy again. But if you talk to me every once in a while I just might say something to make you smile.

Perspective #10

Many times after a divorce we want and need to spend some time alone. Most of us have family or friends that can help us with the children, but many of us do not. If you are the primary care provider it may seem like you never get a chance to get some personal time. Most of your efforts are spent doing what needs to be done to keep everyone and everything on schedule. After a while, if we are not careful, our children become one of those things that need to be done or handled so that we can quickly get to the part of the evening where there is no one up except us.

But the children are not objects that we can shift and shuffle around until everything is accomplished. They need to interact with us on an emotional level, particularly during this transition. In all of our planning and organizing, we can't lose sight of both our children's and our own need to be human with each other.

Lesson #11

"Stop Spending So Much Time Away From Me"

I've heard you say you're tired, you need time to think, or you just gotta get away. Are you trying to get away from your problems or me? Maybe it's the same thing. I know you have to work and go to meetings from time to time, and I know you want to spend time with your friends and all. But, I really want to see more of you now rather than less. I'm still trying to find a way to feel safe again and I've begun to feel better knowing that one of you is still always around and I can reach the other almost anytime I want to.

But, you go out way more than you used to and leave me here by myself with some older kid. Or you take me over to someone else's house just so you can go shopping or out to dinner. I like to go out to dinner, too. If you take me with you, I promise to behave myself and not make a mess or get too loud. I like hanging-out with you. Even though I know you can't talk to me about everything that is on your mind, what I have to say just might help you forget about it for a little while.

Perspective #11

After all our efforts to keep things moving forward for our children and ourselves, we need to get out into social situations again. We need to interact with other adults and explore new interests.

But since our children are dealing with a greater degree of complexity in the healing process, we have to be sensitive to their need to spend more rather than less time with us. One parent is already gone a majority of the time. So as primary caregivers, we have to make special efforts to balance our need for socialization and our children's need for our presence.

It's often easier on the child if we reserve our outings to times when they are with the other parent, or to times when they can be watched by close family or friends. If we have a need to be out at other times, we can try to make sure it's with a sitter they are very familiar with. On frequent occasions it's useful to take a break together. A picnic, movie or dinner out is a great way to reassure our children that their bond to us is still intact.

Lesson #12

"I Need Friends, And I Want Them To Like You"

Guess what? I'm finding new friends that I can talk to, too. They're really nice and they understand how I feel about things. We hang out at school and on the bus. I like going to their houses to visit. I would love for them to come spend time here with us. Once you meet them, I know you'll like them as much as I do.

But I have just one problem. Will you promise to talk and be nice to them? You don't have to spend too much time with me when they're around. But I think they'd really like you if they saw your smile. When they're around, I want them to see all the reasons why I love you because I want them to love you, too.

Perspective #12

Our children are resilient and will find their own ways to get on with life. Though their healing process is made more complex than ours by the fact that they have the added pressure of going through that brief period called childhood, they will find ways to get on with it.

New friendships seem to help quite a bit. They don't necessarily make the concerns go away, but they alleviate some of the pressure our children may be feeling. Children are committed to the family concept. So bringing home a new friend who makes them feel better is their way of sharing that same "therapy" with us. If nothing else, we can appreciate the gesture and let them know we are happy that they are finding their own social outlets and building new bonds. We reinforce our relationships with our children when we show kindness and attention to the people they care about.

Lesson #13

"My Disobedience Is Sometimes Just My Frustration"

Things have been really tight around here since you two broke up. You get angry more easily and you always look so serious. Sometimes, I'm scared when I'm around you because I want to be careful not to do anything to set you off. That's why I try to hang-out in my room with my things. But worse than that, you promise to do things for me and you don't do them. Either you forget or have some excuse as to why you can't.

Your broken promises and your anger get to be a bit much. You won't let me do anything, and you don't come through for me! So, if I can get away with it, I pretend I don't hear you when you call or tell me to do something. When I can't get away with it, I respond to you the way you respond to me, screaming, stomping and kicking. Enough, already! I don't want to disobey you, but I can only deal with so much. I just want us to be happy with each other.

Perspective #13

It's so easy to become self-absorbed post-divorce. This happens, I suppose, because it sometimes requires intense focus to overcome pain and rejection. As a result, we may try to control our outside environment as much as possible so that our focused efforts are not disturbed. We don't want any unnecessary movement and we don't want to spend time doing anything we did not plan to do. On the other hand, we want to agree to our children's reasonable requests. But when it's time to deliver it just doesn't seem to fit into the schedule.

As a result, we end up making promises we do not keep or we don't allow our children to do things, even around the house, that children of their ages should be allowed to do. Because our children are human just like we are they are likely to respond in kind. How many times have we looked at our children and blamed the other children in their school for negatively impacting their attitudes? The truth is that our children are a reflection of us. If we don't keep our word, they learn to be unreliable. If we act out our anger on them, they will act out their anger on us and others. This is a hard thing to accept, especially when you have a need to release your own frustration. But our children are not the vehicles for that. Their childhood needs to be protected from our insecurities and aggressions. None of this experience is their fault. As adults, we are expected to have the maturity to exercise self-control. If we interact peacefully with our children, they will learn how to interact peacefully with us and others.

Lesson #14

"I Depend On You To Help Me Grow"

Hey, I'm just a kid. Even though I tell you I already know everything, I know that I don't. Oh sure, I walk around confidently and repeat back some of the lessons you've taught me just to prove I know what to do. But, honestly, I don't. When you correct me, I don't like it at first. But after a while I feel good because I now know how far I can go with new things. I really appreciate your help because it teaches me how far I can go before dropping off the edge of a cliff.

What's scaring me now is that you're so distracted with this divorce that you no longer stop me every time I go too far. Even the stuff you used to stop me from doing you say nothing about now. Sometimes I do things that I know are wrong just to see if you care enough to correct me. When you don't, I feel like I'm not that important to you. But you are the one I look to for advice. I see lots of new things every day and I don't know what to do with it all. If you don't tell me what to do with it, who will? So, in spite of how badly you feel from time to time, I need you to be my parent all of the time.

Perspective #14

Everyone is bombarded with thousands of pieces of data every day. Our minds instinctively weed out some of what we don't need. For the rest, we have to learn to be selective. As adults, we have learned through experience how to manage both internal and external information. So whether it's a divorce or some other traumatic experience we are pretty good at taking what we want from the information we're exposed to and walking away from the rest.

Children, on the other hand, are just learning how to do that. It is the role of the parent to teach them how. What we teach our children about right and wrong is what helps them as adults make right decisions. It's a process that continues from infancy to adulthood. But after a traumatic experience, children need much more guidance in making the right choices. As hard as it may be to press past your own feelings to attend to the needs of your child, you must to do it so you don't put their future at greater risk.

Lesson #15

"I Love To Help Out, But…"

We're a team now. When things changed, I gladly stepped up to help fill in the hole that was left. I know I'm not big enough to completely fill those shoes, but I feel I have to do more than I used to. That's why sometimes I'll clean up after myself without your asking or I'll put my things together for school all by myself. I enjoy working with you to sweep the floors, load the washing machine and do the dishes.

But there is some stuff I just can't do! I like to vacuum the floor but I can't do it as well as you want it done. I can't fold my clothes like you do, wash out the tub like you do or even clean up my room as well as you do. I know you can use the extra help now that one of you is gone, but I'm just not the one. Maybe one of your friends can help from time to time. Maybe you're too embarrassed to ask for their help. You know, I like a really clean house, too. But maybe we can do a little less so that we can spend the extra time having fun with each other.

Perspective #15

Help can sometimes be hard to come by when you're a primary caregiver. Having to do it all on your own can be challenging; if you never had sympathy for a single parent before, divorce will give it to you. I think that's one of the reasons many of us jump right back into another relationship before weighing all the costs.

Our children love to help out especially when they see we are in need. Even in a setting where the parents are still married, children want to participate in the home by helping us do what we do. If they're pretty good at it, we may be tempted to allow them to share the load left by the departure of our former partners. However, there is a limit to what they should reasonably be responsible for. Their helping out around the house is a training mechanism we can use to help them become responsible adults. So their chores should be measured out according to age and maturity. It is not up to them to fill in the "need" for another adult. I have observed that when children are expected to do more than they reasonably should, it has a negative impact on their sense of responsibility when they become adults. Burned-out children can often turn into irresponsible and immature adults.

Lesson #16

"I Depend On You To Be There For Me"

There's a reason why I can't be considered an adult before I turn 18. Sometimes, though, I wish I could be so that I could make my own decisions and do exactly what *I* want. If I could, I would go to school when I got ready, wear whatever I wanted, eat what I wanted and, definitely, stay up all night until *I* wanted to go to bed.

But the real truth is that the world is a scary place. It's a lot bigger than me. I often wonder how you know everything that you know. You seem to handle the world just fine, outside of the times you're unhappy. But even then, you seem to pull it back together without anyone telling you it's going to be all right. I don't know how to do that. There are so many questions on my mind about how things work, and there are new things I see and don't understand every day. You're the only one I want to look to for help because I trust you. I can't solve my own problems or answer my own questions. I depend on you to help me figure it all out. I know it's tough trying to decide exactly how we are all going to move forward with life. But I need you to be there for me when I can't figure my life out for myself.

Perspective #16

With so much going on, the last thing we want to do is take on more responsibility. As a matter of fact, if we could reduce some of the responsibilities we already have we just might be able to hold our head above water. But the parenting function cannot be considered when looking for ways to save time or reduce costs.

Parenting even in a married relationship can be demanding if done well. This is because children will consistently have great needs, even outside the issues surrounding a divorce. We owe it to our children to be responsive to their needs both concerning and not concerning the divorce.

You will find the strength to continue. I believe that if we can make maintaining and strengthening our family connections the focus of our healing efforts, the process will go much quicker and be more successful for everyone.

Lesson #17

"Please, Do Something Other Than Work"

We don't get to see each other very much with you at work and me at school most of the day. So, I look forward to getting home and seeing you. Home is where I'm most comfortable. There's no pressure and I don't have to worry about whether or not anybody likes me or will want to stay my friend. But when we get home you go right back to work. You change your clothes, throw me some dinner, clean the house, yell at me about my homework and send me off to bed! This is not exactly what I look forward to at the end of each day.

I was hoping we could spend some real time talking about what went on in each other's day and maybe share a few laughs about stuff that's not necessarily all that funny but funny enough so we can laugh together. I need to talk to you because that's how I reconnect to what's comfortable after having spent the day with people I really don't know all that well. I don't require too much of your time. Just a little bit more than I'm getting now.

Perspective #17

The world moves and changes so fast that we have accelerated everything in our lives in order to keep up. Children don't necessarily understand the need for speed. Nor do they want their quality time with us sacrificed for getting things done quicker, better and easier.

They cling to and want to interact with us because they are trying to learn all the things that they think we know. They need our insight into their experiences, and to them, we are the ultimate voice of reason and wisdom.

Lesson #18

"Please Sit Down And Eat Dinner With Me"

We have our table. You have your tray. When you tell me to set the table I would put down enough forks for all of us. But then you do it. You put my food down, watch me start eating and then fix your own plate. As you walk away from the counter I wonder, "will you or won't you, tonight?" Almost all of the time I notice you won't. So, I started asking when I set the table whether or not you'd be joining me. Your answers have mostly been, "not." Now, I don't even have to ask. I just pick up one less fork.

If we can find anything to enjoy doing together, eating is it. You like food; I like food. You get hungry; I get hungry. You like what you cook; I tolerate what you cook ("just kidding"). Eating together is the one time we can all do the same thing, at the same time and in the same place. If it's ever clear that you don't want to spend time with me, it's at dinner-time. There's no good excuse for this one. We all have to eat and it's not hard for us to do it together. Do you really prefer listening to the news or watching your favorite show to talking to me for a mere 30 minutes? I know you say it's what helps you to relax. But what's relaxing to me is being close to you, touching your hand and sharing a smile.

Perspective #18

Allow me to share my personal experience here. Trying to get it all done and keep it all together with two children after a divorce when you never planned on doing it alone can be downright exhausting. I've worked all day, picked the children up, fixed their food and watched them eat it. But when I've felt so exhausted, only a few activities are relaxing: eating, showering and sleeping.

I prefer to sit quietly and enjoy a good meal, not exactly what you get when you sit down to eat with two small children. Between complaining about what they like and don't like and using the unwanted food for things you couldn't even imagine, eating at the same table at the same time can be hair-raising!

But it is one of many sacrifices I had to make in order to let them know that I care deeply for them and value spending time with them. It also does wonders towards teaching them good table manners.

Lesson #19

"I Want To Spend Less Time With Babysitters"

I don't like it when you go away or go out so frequently. But I do understand that you need time to yourself and time with your friends. I even understand the times you have to go away for long weekends. I just have one request. If you have to be gone for a long time and even out for a long night, can I please stay with the other of you?

Babysitters are fun for a while. But with you gone as much as you are I'd much rather live with someone I know and feel really comfortable with. I mean, we live in the same city and all. Can you both work it out so I can stay with one of you? It seems like all my friends get to stay at home with their parents or grandparents. And when their parents go away they get to go with them. Their parents really look out for them. Like I said, I understand if you can't take me with you. But at least leave me with one of you so I can feel that you want to stay connected to me like I want to stay connected to you.

Perspective #19

Hopefully, as a primary care giver, you don't have to spend much time out of town. But for many of us, the occasional business trip or late night meeting is inevitable. It may seem easier not to try to work a childcare schedule out with our former partners, especially if they seem less than reasonable.

But for the child's sense of stability in this newly-divided family it is best if we all can sacrifice to help each other during the times when one of us needs to be away. In reality, we are not doing it for each other. The times when I have had to be away, it broke my heart to have to leave my children with someone other than my former partner. I believe that children, especially young ones, should always feel as though they are at home, and I believe they get the greatest sense of that when they are with at least one of their parents.

So when considering whether or not to avail ourselves for our former partners when they need to be out of town, imagine how our children may feel if they have to stay with someone other than us.

Lesson #20

"Please Don't Yell At Me When I Make Mistakes"

Nobody's perfect. (I heard that somewhere before). That's especially true of me. Most of the time I can do things pretty well. But sometimes I don't quite hit the mark. I'm not downing myself, but the truth is no matter how hard I try I can't do everything right or well enough to make you happy with me. I get so tired of trying that now I'm choosing not to do anything at all. I can't get into trouble for doing nothing, right?

You used to be more patient with my mistakes by saying it was okay and showing me how to do things the right way. But now, one little misplaced shoe or chair not pushed under the table and you lay into me like I burned the house down! I've gotten a little tougher through this process, but your yelling really shakes me and makes me question whether this time is the time you're gonna call it quits with me. You know, like it was with the two of you before the divorce. I always breathe a sigh of relief after you've calmed down and go back to treating me like "normal." But I still worry that the next time may be the last time.

Perspective #20

Self-control is never needed more than when we are tired, frustrated, and have responsibility for others. It is too easy to take out our feelings on others when they do something we do not expect or do not want them to do.

But our children are not responsible for their current circumstances. Together, we and our former partners built a life that included dependent human beings; and together, for whatever reasons, we decided to break down that structure in order to go out and rebuild our own. In the process of making that decision many of us did not yet fully understand what impact it would have on our children and how we were supposed to assist them through it.

The key to coming up with right solutions for our families is to recognize that WE have the responsibility for THEM. Children are not responsible for making sure they are perfect so as not to upset us any further. We are responsible for ensuring they have as "normal" a life as possible, in spite of our decision to divorce.

Lesson #21

"I'm Loud When I Play Because That's What Kids Do"

I've kinda given up trying to help you solve all of this, and I get the feeling you really don't want my help. That's actually kind of a relief because there are other things I'd rather be doing. I want to have fun. If I can't laugh with you, I can laugh with my friends or at my videos. When I have fun I like to get every part of me involved, my arms, my legs and especially my voice. It feels really good when I can laugh loudly and scream at the top of my lungs!

At home is when I'm most free. I don't have to sit quietly and listen to a teacher for hours upon hours, and I don't have to walk in straight lines behind other people just to get from one place to another. At home, I like to let loose and let it all hang out. Now, apparently, you don't share my appreciation for youthful expression. If my voice gets a few notches above normal, you're telling me to pipe down. If I run a little through the house, you yell at me to walk. Don't touch the walls, no feet on the furniture and definitely no jumping on the bed. I know we need rules for every situation, but I need a little more freedom here at home. I know you can't take the noise like you used to because you have so much more to do and to think about. But I can't take the strictness. I need to know that, if nowhere else, I'm free to be me at home.

Perspective #21

In jointly bearing the responsibility for the well being of our children after divorce, our efforts should center on helping them enjoy as normal a childhood as possible. The new homes we create should reflect children's needs as well as our own. We can't now make that bachelor pad we always wanted or have that quaint, beautifully decorated woman's lair that we've always dreamed of because technically we are not single. We are still married to our children. As much as we thought divorce meant we were going to be free to do everything we missed out on doing while we were married, in fact we are still in a situation where we have to live with consideration for others.

Now, more than ever, our children's requirements need to be incorporated into our new way of doing things. This need is rooted in their need to be reassured of their family connection. They can't just live in y*our* house or sit on y*our* sofa. Everything common needs to be ours, with everyone respecting the provisions that have been made. So, although we could not find a way to effectively compromise with our former partners in marriage, we have to find a way to live cooperatively with our children.

Lesson #22

"Please Say Yes, Sometimes"

Most things I don't even have to ask you about anymore. The answer is always the same. No, you can't go play with your friends, No, you can't play with that game right now, No, you can't do *anything* you want to do. Not only do you say "no" almost all the time, there is usually no good reason for saying it. I can get half way into doing something and you say no. You don't even know what it was I was going to do!

Do you know what it feels like to be told no all the time? It makes me feel like every thought I have is wrong. I question every move I make. Should I try to pick up these papers I dropped on the floor? Should I get dressed now or wait for you to tell me to? Should I clean up after myself? I feel like this is stuff I should do but I also feel a little unsure of myself when it comes to doing things on my own. Now, I feel like I have to make a decision in order to get rid of this confusion. Either I sit around and wait for you to tell me every little thing to do, or I ignore you and do what I think is best. But, I don't want to ignore you because I know I don't know everything, yet. If you could say no just when you have to and say yes when it doesn't really matter, I will feel better about me.

Perspective #22

I guess the central theme of these perspectives is sacrifice and compromise. All the things we couldn't figure out how to do in our marriages we remain obligated to figure out with our children.

Healthy children need to learn balance. They can't be told "yes" to everything but they certainly should not hear "no" all the time. It is easier for us as parents to say no because a yes typically obligates us to participate in some way. But in an effort to spare our children a future in which they are dysfunctional or immature as adults, we must sacrifice enough time and energy to allow them experiences that will make them better people in the long run.

Lesson #23

"Let Me Know When I Do A Good Job"

I know you have no problem letting me know when I do things the wrong way. But what about the times I do things right, and not only right, but really well? Sometimes I'm so proud of myself when I look at the things I can do. When I try to show you what I've done, you're either too busy or you act like it's no big deal. Since you know more than me, if you think it's no big deal then maybe I shouldn't think it's such a big deal either.

But on the other hand, I'm getting fairly comfortable with me. I think I'm really learning how to tell the difference between what's good and what's bad. Besides, I like the way I feel when I think I've done a good job. So, I think I'll just go with that. You probably don't get excited for me because you're too busy dealing with other things. I want to value your opinion but you just don't seem to have time to give it. Up to this point, everything I've done was my way of trying to please you. I don't want to stop caring about how you feel, so please let me know when I've done a good job.

Perspective #23

Praise is powerful reinforcement for adults as well as children. And children are always looking to us for a reason to feel good. Having experienced divorce, they need reasons to believe the future is worth moving toward. The last thing we want is for them to look for positive reinforcement outside of the home. Because of their innate drive to survive, they will do what they have to in order to find support. They want to find that support in us and they will try various things to get it until they've reached their own limit. Married or divorced, our parenting must include the appropriate balance of praise and correction.

Lesson #24

"Remember That I Have Needs, Too"

I think I've been pretty patient with you throughout this whole process. I know you're both hurting and working through it in your own separate ways. I don't like the distance I feel from you, but I think it's because you're still sad. I understand your need to heal your sadness and find a way to move on with life. But in all your healing there's just one little area you've overlooked. Me. I feel like I'm competing with your sadness for attention.

Grown ups aren't the only ones that need healing. As a matter of fact, I actually may need more than you do. Not only am I hurt, but I'm also confused. Not only am I confused; I didn't even see this coming. It was a total shock to me. One day you were both here with me, the next, one was here and the other was there. On top of all of that, I'm still going through drastic changes that automatically come with being a kid. This is not the time to zone-out on me. I need your support as much as you need mine. I need your guidance as much as you need my obedience. I need you to attend to me as much if not more than you attend to your own needs.

Perspective #24

One of the best ways I've found to heal is to focus on someone other than myself. When I observe the human condition throughout the world and in my own country, personal traumas don't seem so significant.

As we are trying to find our strength and regain our bearings, we may more easily achieve those goals by focusing on the corporate healing of our families. Taking time to check in with our children to see how things are progressing can help resolve stagnant issues and lead to non-divorce related conversations that strengthen our connections.

Lesson #25

"I Want You To Try To Work It Out"

You know how you're always telling me to talk things out with my friends and make up? You know how you are always encouraging me to share or compromise in order to make peace? Why can't the two of you do the same thing? In my mind, you're both good people. You're nice, loving and good-looking, too. So, what's the problem?

I've heard you say it's impossible and you've tried everything but nothing works. But are you sure you've looked at *every*thing? I want to make sure you really have done your very best to make this work. I think it would be easier for everybody if you did. You wouldn't have to pack my things so I can go away every week and I wouldn't have to tell the same stories more than once. Although I've gotten used to the separation, I still hold out hope that some day you'll figure it out and we'll all be together again. Being with both of you is my greatest wish.

Perspective #25

It may seem like everyone is adjusting to the change brought about by your divorce. The children may seem like they're getting back to normal and you may begin to date new people.

But I believe that, except in the most violent of cases, every child wants his or her parents to get back together some day. Who wouldn't want the two people they love most in the world to love each other? Our children may become accustomed to the change, but their hearts may always hold out hope for the manifestation of their dream.

Lesson #26

"Work It Out Or Work Together"

In my dreams I imagine us all together again. But since it seems like that will never happen, the least you can do is stop fighting with each other about who's going to take care of me. I get tired of hearing from each of you about how bad the other one is. When I hear these things I feel so confused because I don't know you like that.

Sometimes you forget that I don't know how to handle the kind of information you handle. When I get confused, I don't know if I can trust either of you anymore. I feel like someone is lying to me but which one of you is it? I don't want to have to figure this out and I don't want to feel these bad feelings I have when you complain in front of me. You don't have to keep fighting with each other, especially over me. Didn't you get divorced so you could stop fighting? Whatever you decide to do is all right with me. Just agree to do something and stop arguing about it.

Perspective #26

Some couples find a way to put it back together even after an extended separation. But most of us do not. Where there are two relatively mature adults, efforts can be made to be cordial and cooperative with regard to the children.

Children absorb information every day, and because of our connection they absorb more quickly the information they glean from our behaviors and interactions. As part of our sacrifices for their sakes we have to control our urges to argue with our former partners in our children's hearing, particularly if it concerns them. Nothing dampens joy and happiness faster than watching people you love tear each other down. If you're divorced now, hopefully you have worked through how you're going to properly care for your children. But they don't need to be privy to those discussions and interactions. Our primary concern should be to guard their hearts until they are mature enough to guard their own.

Lesson #27

"Too Much Change Really Scares Me"

I'm trying to be strong. Really, I am. When one of you left I felt so alone and scared. But then almost everything I was used to began to change. The house was emptier, you started acting differently, you started treating me differently and basic things seemed to get harder to do. I see more babysitters than ever and you're introducing me to new people all the time. Now you're telling me we may have to move to another house and I may have to go to another school.

I'm terrified! All I want to do is enjoy being a kid and grow up. Do you know how hard it is to make new friends? What will the new school bus be like? What will my new teacher be like? Will I feel safe in our new house? Will it be as nice as this one? I'm so scared and I can't do anything about it. Why can't I just stay here? Maybe I can go stay with grandma. Nothing ever changes at her house. Do we have to do all of this right now? All this change really scares me. Please, if we don't have to move, let's not.

Perspective #27

Even adults don't like a lot of change. However, in many divorce situations we want to just wipe the slate clean and start fresh with everything.

But our children may not be able to handle that given their relationships with both partners. Our problems with our former partners are not necessarily their problems with those partners. While we may want a completely new environment and new things, our children may need to hold on to some of the old environment in order to survive the transition.

Some changes have to be made, but think about which things you can keep the same for your child so their loss won't feel as great.

Lesson #28

"Sometimes I Feel It Is My Fault"

I keep trying to figure this all out and how it went wrong. I don't see where it's either of your faults. So whose fault is it? Someone has to be to blame, don't they? When I think back and I see how angry you've been with me and how you ignore me from time to time, I wonder if it's me.

I really think it might be my fault when you argue over me or say you wouldn't even be bothered with each other if it weren't for me. I know you've told me over and over this has nothing to do with me. But from what I can see and hear it seems to have everything to do with me. I wish I could undo what I did wrong so things would be right again. Maybe I need to stop thinking about this because it makes me feel so sad. I wish I could understand what went wrong.

Perspective #28

Most of us have a good sense of how much information our children can handle. Even from the first communication with them regarding divorce, we try to present the news in a way that we think will be least traumatic.

They may not ever say it or show clearly visible signs of it, but many children feel that they have contributed to the breaking of the marriage. We see divorce as the breakdown of an adult relationship; our children view it as a breakdown of the entire family. Having picked up the message through experience that every wrong event must be someone's fault, they naturally might turn to themselves. They don't necessarily see anything wrong in either parent, so the tendency is to think it is them.

I have found that a key to resolving this issue is honest communication, even with young children. You might simply explain that when people marry they hope it is forever, but sometimes, adult circumstances are such that no matter how hard they've tried, it was in everyone's best interest that the adults no longer stay together. Letting the child know you still get along and communicate may also help them overcome feelings of guilt.

Lesson #29

"Please Let Me Know That You Still Love Me"

In spite of all the really rough times we've had, I still love you. I look up to both of you and depend on you for just about everything. The question still in my mind is do you love me? I tell myself that you do because you take care of me and let me stay with you. But I really never hear you say it or see it through a smile.

You're still tuned out to me most of the time and I can never catch your eyes to let you know I'm thinking of you. I've really felt like I've gone through a lot of this divorce alone. So, I don't expect to hear you say you love me. But I keep hoping that one day you'll break through your sadness and let me know that I mean the world to you and that you love me more than anything.

Perspective #29

If the lack of communication helped to kill your marriage, it can also destroy your relationship with your children.

Children, especially, deserve to be reinforced with verbal and physical expressions of affection. Adults can rationalize, based on an analysis of all the information presented to them, that they are liked or disliked. Children on the other hand may take one piece of negative information and form a judgment.

I believe it is vital to our families' health that we continuously express love for each other in word and in action.

Lesson #30

"I Want To Know That You're All Right"

You know what's kept me going through all of this? The fact that you need me. I'm afraid of what might happen if I weren't here to look out for you, protect you, and make sure you're doing okay. You're a part of me, and when you hurt, I hurt.

I look in your face and I wish I could make the hurt go away. I still try to think of ways to help you because it worries me when you stay sad for so long. I do my best to be a friend to you by helping you with whatever I can. I try to talk to you about the every day so you can get your mind off things for a while. But I don't think you're letting me in because I'm just a kid. Well, if you don't respond to me, I wish you'd respond to someone. I need to know that you're going to be all right, if not today then some day real soon.

Perspective #30

We all know that healing is a process and from time to time we may slip back into a sad memory. Although they may seem to be selfish at times, most children will step up with tons of love and compassion if they think we need their help.

They are willing to exhaust themselves to help us if they think it will make a difference. But whether they do it or someone else does it, they just want to see us get better. Being sensitive to their sensitivity to us is important. Responding to let them know we are all right may help alleviate the burden they feel. For, a child who worries for weeks or months at a time may suffer significant harm that impacts other areas of their lives. At the same time, it is important that we take appropriate action to help ourselves so that they can see our improvement. Corporate healing includes us.

Lesson #31

"I Need To Be Reassured, Constantly"

I'm doing my best to hold it all together. For your sake, I act like I'm just fine and I don't need much. Actually, I'm so concerned about you that I don't think about myself much anymore. But when I come to the end of my energy, I want you to hold me, and I try to find the words to say I just need you to love me.

I think it would be wrong to ask so much for myself when you carry so much, already. But I really need to know that I'm okay and I'm doing what I'm supposed to be doing. Can we find a way for you to let me know I'm where I should be without it being a big hassle for you? Maybe you could give me a smile and a pat on the shoulder once a week? I just need you to give me a little of yourself so that I know I'm becoming who I should become.

Perspective #31

We need to keep checking in with our children. It's important to ask them how they feel about life in general and what their everyday experiences are like. We also need to let them know that we, too, are doing well with our recovery.

It can be easy to overlook this need when it seems like things have become normal again. But as a good parenting skill, communicating in a friendly conversation with our children is vital to strengthening the family bond.

Lesson #32

"We Don't Need To Spend Money To Have A Lot Of Fun"

I know what we all need. A night of family fun! So what, we're not all together? We can still do things that will make us happy. Maybe if we focus on having fun with each other we'll find a way to forget all our problems. I know money is tighter now with just one of you. But we don't need to spend money to have a lot of fun.

I can make up games for us to play. We can have a singing contest and play music together, or we can read books together and maybe even write one. Anything, anywhere with you would be lots of fun.

Perspective #32

One of the most valuable things we can start doing after a divorce is to start living again. Holding on to bitterness and anger doesn't hurt the other partner, but it hurts our children and us. For many, divorce also negatively impacts our finances for a while, making it more difficult to participate in outside activities.

But in an effort to rebuild our families and ourselves, we can take time to do free activities that families do. Even as the only parent, we can include other family members or close friends in activities that reinforce a sense of togetherness and reliability.

Our children will learn from our example of healing how to resolve and move on from issues in their own lives. For our sake and theirs, we should keep our eyes on building a brighter future with a small rear-view mirror to the past to ensure we don't take wrong turns up ahead.

Lesson #33

"More Family Can Be A Good Thing If…"

More changes and more new people. Now you're telling me that this new person is going to live with you, us. I'm not sure how I feel about it. I still have hope that the two of you will get back together. But since I dream of that less and less, explain to me how this new thing is supposed to work.

Okay, I guess it can be a good thing if,

1. I never lose either of you.
2. This new person is coming to add happiness not problems.
3. They never try to separate us.
4. They love me and treat me as nicely as you do.

It feels good to know we're adding to each other, again instead of taking away.

Perspective #33

One of the things we dread most about divorce is when our former partners find other mates, especially before we do. After we get over wondering how anyone else could get into a relationship with them knowing all that we know, we have to figure out how the new expanded family is going to work for all of us.

I believe wholeheartedly in getting to know, at some level, the new stepparent. Why? The children will now be learning some of their values from them. I also adhere to the notion that all parties should work together to ensure the child has a sense of expanded relationships rather than loss.

Taking time and being sure before entering into a new commitment is also important. No child should have to experience the loss of divorce a second time. The still-single parent should try to be gracious and supportive of the former partner's new relationship, so that the child doesn't have to overcome unnecessary barriers to making this new connection.

Lesson #34

"We Are All Still Family"

I know you've both gone your own way and you're adding new things to your new lives. But I am still forever committed to both of you. No matter what happens we will always be connected. In my mind, even though we live in separate places we're all still family.

Now that you have found other people to make you happy, you seem to get along better. Maybe not right away, but let's all get together for a picnic or something. I want you to meet each other's new friends. You have to see each other anyway when you're dealing with me. So we might as well enjoy it. I like the way family feels. I'm so proud and happy to have so many people interested in what happens to me. It means so much to have all of you care and spend time with me.

Perspective #34

As much as possible, parents should work to ensure that there is a fluid sense of family. One in which the child feels as though there is one set of connections that transcends two marital relationships. Both couples don't have to spend large amounts of time together, even though I've seen it done quite successfully. But mature adults can find ways to get along not only to help the child feel secure but to set an example of forgiveness and cooperation.

Lesson #35

"I Want To Stay With You Forever"

Who else do I have in this world besides you? Who is willing to forgive me when I mess up and hug me at the same time? Who goes out of their way to make sure I have what I need for school, and who else will just take me out for a treat as a surprise? You are so special to me. I admire you because you're strong and you taught me how to be strong. You're kind and you taught me how to be kind.

I don't want anyone else as my parent more than you. Through everything, you never let go of me. So, I just need to let you know that I want to stay with you forever, and wherever you go, I'm going to go.

Perspective #35

One of the things that snapped me out of my remorse and "just get it all done" attitude was when my son hugged my neck while I was tucking him in one night and said "Mommy, I want to stay with you forever, and wherever you go I'm going to go."

It was so unexpected that it made me stop and really start looking at what was going on inside his mind and heart. I'm sure this had an indirect impact on my writing this book. After divorce we tend to think about healing in terms of our feelings and what we went through, and by the way we have to make sure the children are okay, too.

But they're so much more than sideline players in the transition. They are not only a vital component of but are contributors to the healing process. Our children learn much from us, but every day brings great opportunities for us to learn from them.

Lesson #36

"I Love To See You Smile"

I see how hard you've tried to get back on your feet and take care of me at the same time. I just want to say how proud I am of you for finding happiness again. I am comforted by your new smile and to see your eyes meet mine, again. You're more relaxed and you're not as hard on me anymore.

We've all made new friends while keeping some of the old ones, and your happiness lets me feel free to focus on being a kid. When you smile at me or watch me do what I do, I know you care and you're now making sure that *I'm* all right. Even though it's not the same as when you were both here, I can be happy like this with a happy you.

Perspective #36

Often children understand the concept of family better than we do. Truly, when we hurt, they hurt and when we're happy, they're happy. There are times when I read something and laugh and my daughter will come and try to read the same thing and laugh just to laugh with me. Most of the time, she was clueless about what was on the page.

But the point is that our children take cues from us not only in behavior and attitude but in emotion as well. They welcome the opportunity to smile with us and share in whatever makes us glad. Likewise, they want to share their every happy moment with us, and I am now convinced that it is not just for their own sense of gratification. I believe they share their happy experiences because they want us to experience that same happiness for ourselves.

Lesson #37

"Be Patient With Me. I Have A Lot To Figure Out"

My life has changed but I still feel pretty good about things. But how can I feel good without my dream coming true? Life is strange, or is just being a kid strange? I know you like to move fast and get things done with lightning speed. But some things I still need to take slowly.

For example, I understand your need for new friends, really close friends. But I'm still trying to get settled with what that means to our relationship and to me. It must be good for you since you seem so much happier. Yet, where exactly do I fit in to this new picture? I don't think you'll leave me, and I would never let you after all of this. But if you could take the time to explain it to me I would surely appreciate it. Please explain it, don't dictate it.

Perspective #37

I don't know that children, or even adults for that matter, fully get over a divorce. Children may still have lingering questions even after they've accepted it and continued on.

As parents we need to remain sensitive to our children, particularly as they grow and start to form dating relationships of their own. The types of relationships they gravitate to may be an indication of issues unresolved from the divorce.

Communication, affection and persistence are keys to making sure they make healthy life decisions as they progress to adulthood.

Lesson #38

"I May Feel Sad From Time To Time"

We all have our moments. I appreciate everything you've done and how you keep watching out for me. But every once in a while, especially when the other of you is picking me up, I wish it didn't have to be like this. I want to stay at home and have both of you come stay here with me.

I'm used to our new life and I even like different things about it. But there's nothing better than having the two people I love most in the world right here all the time. I wish you liked each other, but I'm not asking anymore. I just want you to understand that I will occasionally slip away into these thoughts in my mind. I'll get over it quickly and keep going, but they will come from time to time.

Perspective #38

Children are little human beings, and some things come naturally to us at any age. Thoughts of the past may bring back feelings we thought were gone long ago.

Children's hopes for our reconciliations may be dormant, but they are still there, hidden inside. Hopefully, they have learned how to manage those hopes so that they are no longer expectations. But part of our role as parents is to ensure that we help them through these reflective periods with reassurance. They need to know that they are still loved by both parents, and that both are working together in friendship to help make their childhoods the best they can be.

Lesson #39

"Always Remember That I Love You More Than Anything Else"

We've come a long way but we made it. We may have setbacks on occasion, but we get back on track rather quickly now. I'm focusing on being a kid, so there are certain things I don't think I need you for anymore. Nothing personal, but I've grown a lot faster than you thought I have.

Yet, one thing has never changed and never will. Both of you are the most important people in the world to me and I will always love you for who you are and who you are trying to be. There is nothing and no one that I love more than both of you. Thanks for loving me, too.

Perspective #39

Adults may fall in and out of what we call love rather quickly. But parents have to work very hard to lose the love of their children. This is because children, who aren't familiar with adult "complexity," know what true love is.

Love transcends emotion and is wrapped in commitment. The moment you told them you were mommy or daddy and you supported that claim with provision, protection and affection, you gained their die-hard commitment to love you forever. Even after you've behaved badly towards them by taking your anger out on them or restricting their behavior unnecessarily, they remain ready to forgive and cling close to you, again.

Unlike adults who have learned through a mindset of mistrust how to bite the hands that feed them, children remain indebted to those who show them kindness. But even beyond all this, it is their desire to remain connected to family that causes them to love us beyond all our faults, hang-ups and insufficiencies. In light of these things, how much more can we do to embrace, cherish and replenish their love?

STOP My Childhood From Drowning!

Conclusion

Children of any age are precious and innocent. The 18 years we have to guide and teach them go by far too quickly, and at the end we hope we have imparted enough value for them to achieve life success that far exceeds our own.

When that growth experience is encumbered with a divorce, parenting and adulthood become far more demanding. How do we continue to sow good seeds into our children's lives while transplanting the roots that have already grown in both them and us? Because they have but a few years to glean from our knowledge and experience before living life for themselves, our approach to healing and progress should be one that fully incorporates the entire family's needs.

What's required in each situation is uniquely dependent on the particular parents and children involved. But in each situation attention to our children's emotional and physical needs is paramount. Nothing is impossible to one who believes. If we have the maturity to marry, have children and make the difficult decision to divorce, we can find ways to rebuild and strengthen our family connections so that everyone, including ourselves, is whole.

STOP My Childhood From Drowning!

Other Products by E.R. Reid

The Proverbs 31 Woman

The Life Area Planner and Journal

**What Does Your Produce Look Like?
How to Live a Purposeful Life**

**STOP My Family From Drowning!
Parental Expressions For A Child
Experiencing Divorce**

**You may obtain information on these and
other products by visiting
www.fruitiononline.com**

or by calling 1-888-80READY

Visit Fruition Online For Helpful Products And Services That Address Your Personal Development and Transition Needs.

FRUITION
WWW.FRUITIONONLINE.COM

"Preparing Minds For Action"

www.fruitiononline.com